Six Weeks to a BRAIN-COMPATIBLE Classroom:

Using Brain Research to Enhance & Energize Instruction

by JANET N. ZADINA, PH.D.

BR&IN
BRAIN RESEARCH
and INSTRUCTION

Contents

The Six-Week Action Plan

From Me to You

Dear Colleagues,

Super-charged, enlightened, energized, empowered, fired-up: those are some of the words educators use to describe how they feel after attending one of my presentations about the brain and learning. That's the purpose of this book—to fire and inspire you to create a brain-compatible classroom that is custom-tailored for your students.

The topic of brain research is a very exciting one for educators. There is an explosion of books on the subject and presenters giving workshops making a link between the research and the classroom. As a former high school and college teacher now engaged in neuroscience research (neuroanatomical risk factors for neurodevelopmental language disorders through MRI brain scans and behavioral interventions for post-traumatic stress disorder), I can see this from the perspective of a scientist and a teacher. I also see a tremendous responsibility to proceed with caution in making these links. My mission is to build a bridge between neuroscience and education for you – a bridge that has integrity but can only carry so much weight at this time. This bridge will grow stronger as we learn more about the brain and as neuroscientists work more with educators.

The new research is exciting and it leads us to think about teaching and learning in new ways and to try new approaches in the classroom. It appears to validate what good teachers have always known, while giving us insight into trying strategies that may help those who learn differently. One thing we can definitely say that the research has shown us is that there is much variety among the brains of individuals and that those who learn differently use their brain differently. Therefore, we want to utilize as much variety in our strategies and approaches as possible to reach the greatest number of individuals.

The work that you do is so important and has an effect on the brains of students. I hope you enjoy this book and KEEP UP THE GREAT WORK.

Janet Zadina

How to Use this Book

Quick Reference

Up front are a few pages of quick "facts" about the brain. You'll notice that I've put quotation marks around the word *facts*. Advances in technology have made it possible for scientists to see inside a living, thinking brain, resulting in an explosion of research. New discoveries continue to render existing textbooks obsolete. For example, just a decade ago, the consensus among neuroscientists was that we are born with all the neurons we will ever have. Now we know that the brain does, in fact, grow new neurons. Some of the information in this workbook may be obsolete in a year or two. That's why it is important to keep abreast of the latest research in neuroscience. That's also why it is important to treat any new research cautiously, since new studies have not yet had time to be replicated. With those caveats in mind, use the Quick Reference section of this workbook to familiarize yourself with the vocabulary and concepts you'll encounter as you implement the brain-compatible strategies inspired by the worksheets in this book.

Six-Week Action Plan

The six-week action plan includes thirty worksheets—five for each week. Of course, it may not be feasible or appropriate for you to use every worksheet in the week. You may want to spread this out over an entire semester. The worksheets are primarily to help you implement some strategies that may be more diversified than you have typically used and to inform you about some of the research on the brain.

Each worksheet has several features:

- **Research:** It is important to realize that much of the research on the brain as it relates to learning has been done on animal models,  particularly rats. Even the research that is done on humans consists of the study of discrete tasks in isolation. There is no direct link to educational practices inherent in this research. However, the research can give us some ideas about how we may make learning more effective.

- **Strategies:** Our practices in the past have been based primarily on behaviorism—practices extrapolated from observations. Now we say we are taking a scientific approach, but we cannot make direct links from a specific study to classroom practice. Once again, we are making inferences, this time from basic science. There is no scientific proof that the strategies work because they haven't been scientifically tested, but the strategies seem appropriate based on what we are learning about the brain. As a teacher, *you* are the expert. You have an instinct for what works and what doesn't work in your classroom. You be the judge.

- **Implementation:** Each worksheet contains space to note what you have done and what you are trying for future reference. You can document the effectiveness of the strategies.

- **CEUs:** Most worksheets contain information about how you can earn continuing education credits by completing the worksheet and related tasks given in this section. These credits would be given by your institution *if* they choose to utilize this workbook in that fashion. The author is not authorized to issue these credits. This is between you and your institution, so check before pursuing this option.

- **The Flipside:** The back of each worksheet contains all sorts of wonderful things for you. Some are forms that you can use to execute tasks. Others are masters that you can photocopy for your students. Some provide additional information or resources. Many of these can be used throughout the year.

The Learning Brain

Plasticity

The brain you have today is not the one you were born with. From the moment you took your first breath, your brain began shaping itself especially for your particular environment. As a human being, your brain possesses more uncommitted cortex than any other species on earth. That gives you an extraordinary capacity for learning. In the presence of an enriched environment, your brain continuously grows new and faster connections. The more connections you grow, the smarter you become. The ability of your brain to change physically in response to learning is called **plasticity**.

How Neurons Connect

When people talk about "gray matter" they are referring to brain cells, or **neurons**. You have at least a hundred billion of them and they work full time transmitting information. The process begins when neurons receive information through their branches, or **dendrites**. If enough signals arrive through the dendrites to stimulate the neuron, it will fire, meaning that it sends the information in the form of electrical pulses down its **axon**. At the end of the axon is a gap, called a **synapse**. The tip of the axon releases chemicals, called **neurotransmitters**, which carry the information across the synapse to the den-

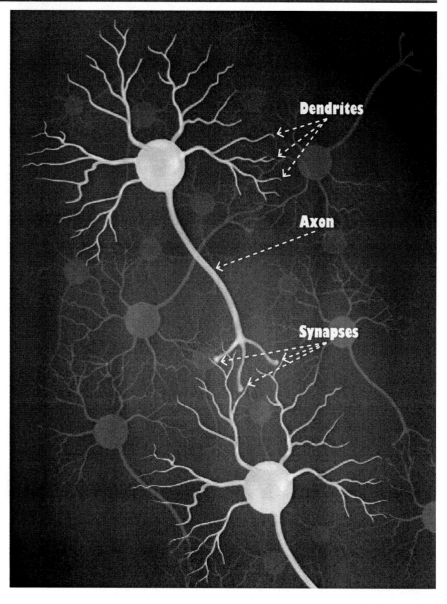

drites of the next neuron. We refer to this process as **firing**.

Transmission

A well-traveled axon is covered in a casing made of a type of white matter, or glia, called myelin. Composed of 80% fat and 20% protein, this myelin sheath increases the speed at which messages travel to the next neuron. A well-myelinated axon results in

faster transmission. Damaged or destroyed myelin can result in diseases like multiple sclerosis and Guillain-Barre syndrome.

> **The key to getting smarter is to make new synaptic connections**

Brain Basics

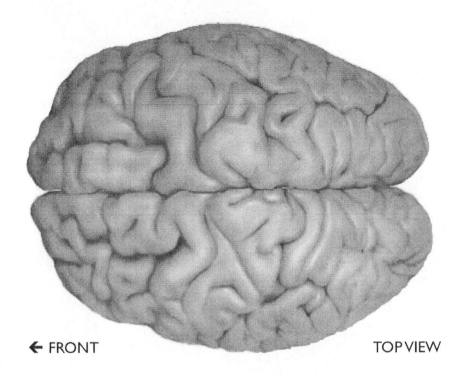

← FRONT   TOP VIEW

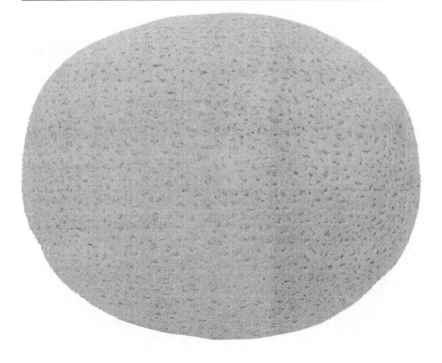

Color
People often refer to the brain as "gray matter." Actually, only 10 percent of the brain consists of gray matter, or **neurons**. The remaining 90 percent is made up of white matter, or **glia** (Greek for "glue"). One type of glial cell forms the myelin sheath, while other glial cells provide support, nutrition, and (see my note).*

Size
Your brain is about the size and weight of a cantaloupe—3 pounds, more or less. That's comparatively large in relation to your body weight. It's high maintenance, too: it requires about 25 percent of your body's fuel and difficult tasks require more fuel.

Texture
Like the cantaloupe, your brain has a "rind." In fact, it's called the **cortex**, which is Latin for "rind" or "bark." But that's where the similarity ends, because the **cerebral cortex** has more wrinkles than a shar-pei. For your brain, wrinkles are an advantage: they increase surface area.

Consistency
The living brain is so soft you could scoop it out with a spoon like mousse. Unlike mousse, however, the brain is mostly water (78%). The remaining ingredients are fat (10%), protein (8%), and other ingredients (4%).

* Stay tuned for updates; glial cells, long regarded as dull and uninteresting, are now the subject of increasing attention.

Brain Geography

Cerebral Cortex

The wrinkly outer covering of your brain is called the **cerebral cortex**. It is the most highly developed—and in evolutionary terms, the newest—of the brain's structures. If you were to spread it out, it would be the size of an unfolded sheet from a daily newspaper (about 50 x 50 inches). Its thickness, however, is more like an orange peel than a sheet of newsprint. The cerebral cortex accounts for about two-thirds of your brain's mass.

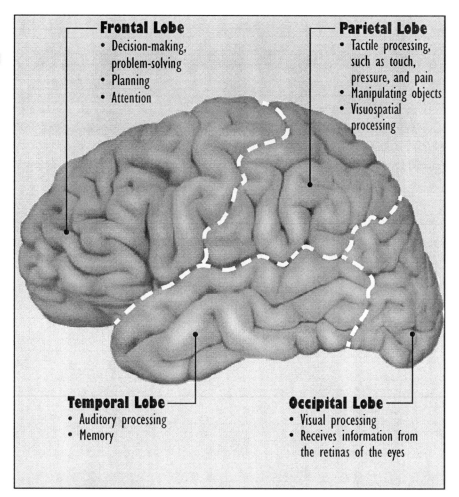

Frontal Lobe
- Decision-making, problem-solving
- Planning
- Attention

Parietal Lobe
- Tactile processing, such as touch, pressure, and pain
- Manipulating objects
- Visuospatial processing

Temporal Lobe
- Auditory processing
- Memory

Occipital Lobe
- Visual processing
- Receives information from the retinas of the eyes

Four Pairs of Lobes

Historically, the cerebral cortex has been divided into four lobes (eight if you count both sides of the brain) that correspond to the bones of the skull by the same names: **frontal**, **temporal**, **parietal**, and **occipital**. Originally, these divisions were purely anatomical. Today, however, scientists are able to associate different functions with the different lobes.

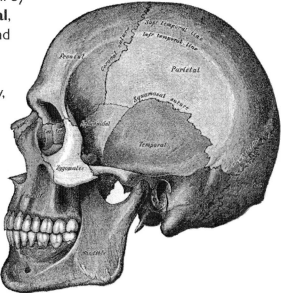

Your frontal lobes, which govern behavior, don't reach full maturity until your early 20s.

From *Gray's Anatomy of the Human Body*, 1918

Left Brain, Right Brain

Lateralization

Your brain has two sides, or **hemispheres**. They are connected by a bundle of fibers called the **corpus callosum**. The left hemisphere controls the right side of your body, while the right hemisphere controls the left side of your body. Also, one side is often dominant, resulting in hand preference. Most people are right-handed (87 percent). Left-handed people represent only 13 percent of the population. Some popular psychologists have taken the right-brain concept further than the research would support, contributing to the false notion that music and art are right-brain frills. Nevertheless, while the hemispheres do cooperate, they do not participate equally in every task. For example, there is convincing evidence that language usually involves the left hemisphere more than the right, while a spatial task, such as reading a map, involves the right brain more than the left. When one hemisphere contributes more to a task than the other, it is called **lateralization**.

Left Hemisphere
- Controls the right side of the body

Right Hemisphere
- Controls the left side of the body

Corpus Callosum
- Connects the two hemispheres

Left Brain Functions	Right Brain Functions
• Sequential	• Simultaneous
• Analytical	• Holistic
• Verbal	• Imagistic
• Logical	• Intuitive
• Perception of counting and measurement	• Perception of shapes and motions
• Grammar and words	• Intonation and emphasis

Key Language Areas

The brain has two key language areas. We know they are key because of what happens if one of them is damaged. For instance, if you suffer damage to **Broca's area**, you cannot speak properly, but you can understand language. On the other hand, if you experience damage to **Wernicke's area**, you cannot comprehend language, but you can speak clearly (even though you will make no sense). Broca's area and Wernicke's area are connected by a bundle of nerve fibers. In a typical scenario, language enters the brain through either the visual cortex (seeing the words) or the auditory cortex (hearing the words). The information travels to Wernicke's area, then to Broca's Area, and finally to the motor cortex (speaking the words), or to the sensory cortex (writing the words).

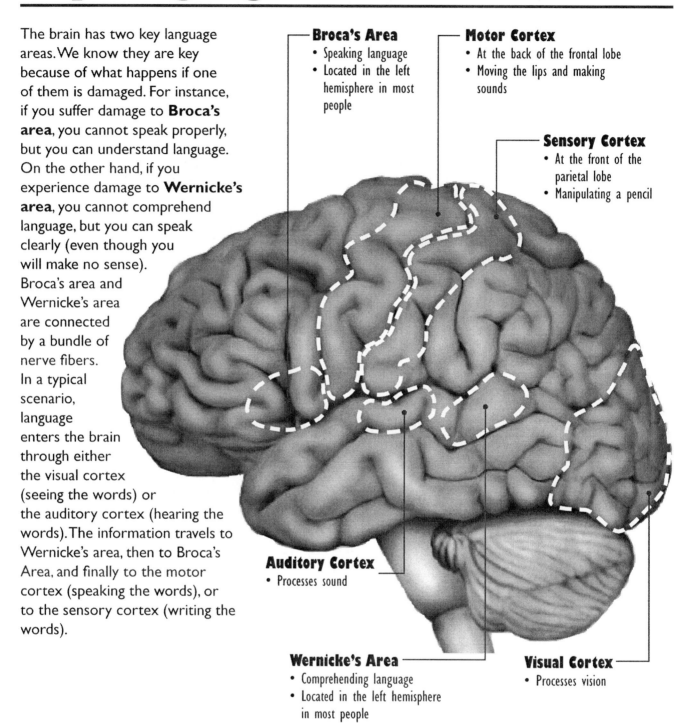

Broca's Area
- Speaking language
- Located in the left hemisphere in most people

Motor Cortex
- At the back of the frontal lobe
- Moving the lips and making sounds

Sensory Cortex
- At the front of the parietal lobe
- Manipulating a pencil

Auditory Cortex
- Processes sound

Wernicke's Area
- Comprehending language
- Located in the left hemisphere in most people

Visual Cortex
- Processes vision

Inside the Brain

The Limbic System

Inside your brain, underneath the wrinkled rind of the cerebral cortex, is the "emotional area," or **limbic system.*** Emotions, sleep, body regulation, hormones, sexuality, and smell are processed in this area. This mid-brain area also produces many of the brain's chemicals. The limbic system includes the thalamus, hypothalamus, hippocampus, and amygdala.

Hypothalamus

- Regulates hunger, thirst, response to pain, levels of pleasure, sexual satisfaction, anger, and aggressive behavior
- Regulates pulse, blood pressure, and breathing

Thalamus

- The gatekeeper for sensory information
- Plays a role in attention

Corpus Callosum

- Connects the two hemispheres

Amygdala

- Two almond-shaped masses of neurons (one in each hemisphere) near the ends of the hippocampi
- Electrical stimulation produces aggression
- Removal causes submissiveness

Hippocampus

- Two "horns" that curve back from the amygdalae (one in each hemisphere)
- Important in converting information into long-term memory
- If your hippocampus is damaged, you cannot build new memories

* Stay tuned for updates; this area, even whether or not it should be called "The Limbic System," is a matter of debate in some scientific circles.

Neuroimaging

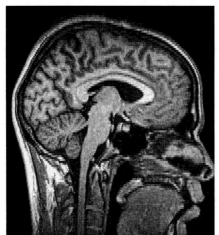

MRI Image from Wikipedia's Creative Commons

▲**MRI**: Magnetic Resonance Imaging (MRI) uses a powerful magnet and radio waves to produce highly-detailed anatomical images. This device is highly useful in detecting abnormalities.

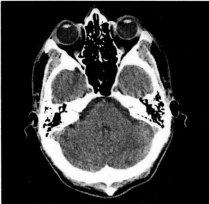

Head CT Scan from Wikipedia's Wikimedia Commons

▲**CT**: Computed tomography (CT) uses a thin X-ray beam to acquire a large series of cross-sections taken around a single axis of rotation. A computer program is then used to generate a 3-D image.

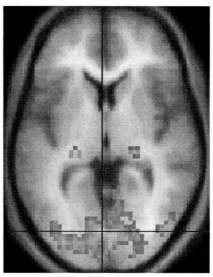

fMRI Image from Wikipedia's Wikimedia Commons

▲**fMRI**: Functional Magnetic Resonance Imaging (fMRI) uses MRI to measure the increase in blood flow to different areas of the brain. When neurons are active, they consume oxygen carried by the blood. The presence of oxygen causes changes in the magnetism of molecules, which are picked up by the device.

EEG: In electroencephalography, electrodes placed on the scalp measure the electrical activity of the brain. The resulting traces are known as an electroencephalogram (EEG). This technique can detect changes on a millisecond time scale. The regions activated are not as specific as fMRI, but it captures time more effectively.

MEG: Magnetoencephalography (MEG) measures the magnetic fields produced by electrical activity in the brain using devices such as superconducting quantum interference devices (SQUIDs).

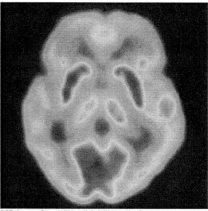

PET Image from Wikipedia's Wikimedia Commons

▲**PET**: Positron Emission Tomography (PET) uses a very small dose of radioactive chemical to detect blood flow, oxygen use, and glucose metabolism. It enables scientists to determine which areas of the brain are activated when the subject performs different activities. An advantage is that PET can show changes at the cellular level, but because it is more invasive, it is not as widely used in research.

SPECT: Single Photon Emission Tomography (SPECT) uses a gamma camera to acquire 2-D images from multiple angles, and then generates true 3-D information using a computer. A tracer is used to assess local brain metabolism and energy use. SPECT can diagnose Alzheimer's disease with as high as 88% accuracy.

Thanks to neuroimaging, scientists can now see inside a living, thinking brain.

Telling Cases

Broca's Area

The area that controls speech is named after the physician who discovered it in 1861. Broca had a patient who, after a stroke, completely lost the ability to speak. The patient could apparently understand language, but the only syllable he could pronounce was "tan," over and over again. After Tan's death, Broca performed an autopsy and determined the site of the stroke. That relatively small area in the left hemisphere is called **Broca's area**.

Wernicke's Area

The area that controls speech comprehension is named after Karl Wernicke, a German neurologist and psychiatrist who, in 1874, discovered that damage to this area could cause a type of aphasia in which a person speaks with a normal syntax, but makes no sense. **Wernicke's area** is connected to Broca's area by a neural pathway.

The Brain and ESOL

Pat Kuhl at the University of Washington in Seattle found that Japanese infants can easily distinguish between American English "r" and "l" sounds. After a certain age, however, if there was no exposure to those sounds, the children no longer differentiated them. Kuhl went on to show that the loss of differentiation can be prevented by very early social interaction with speakers of other languages, but not by recordings. Neuroimaging reveals that Japanese speakers activate only one area when hearing "l" and "r" whereas English speakers activate two areas.

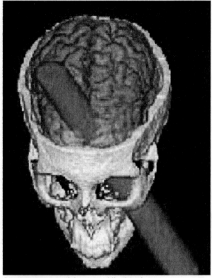
Computer-generated image, public domain

▲Phineas Gage

Phineas Gage was one lucky railroad worker. Or was he? A 3-foot-long iron rod blew through his head with such force that it landed almost 30 yards behind him. Not only did he survive, but he was ready to go back to work within a few months. Unfortunately, his behavior had changed so dramatically that his former employers would not give him back his job. His friends complained that he had become temperamental and unsociable and his doctor described him as fitful, irreverent, and obstinate. The rod had damaged Gage's frontal lobes, which we now know play an important role in behavior.

The Lobotomy

Imagine destroying someone's prefrontal cortex on purpose! In the U.S., 40,000 people were subjected to lobotomies. The most famous was JFK's sister, Rosemary Kennedy. Rarely performed today, the surgery results in the loss of executive functions.

Neurogenesis

Elizabeth Gould of Princeton University overturned a central tenet of neuroscience that you are born with all your neurons. She confirmed earlier findings by Altman and Kaplan that the brain actually creates new neurons. Now she is studying how stress damages the brain. When she and post-doctorate student Christian Mirescu deprived newborn rats of their mother for either 15 minutes or three hours a day, there was a dramatic decrease in **neurogenesis** in the rats' adult brains and a permanent reduction in the number of new cells in the hippocampus. The adult rats may have forgotten their trauma, but their brains didn't.

The Wada Test

In the Wada Test, one side of the brain is anesthetized while the other remains awake. Usually performed before brain surgery, doctors interview the side that is awake. The Wada Test confirms that in 95% of right-handed people and 70% of left-handed people, language resides in the left hemisphere. Another interesting finding involves emotion. When the left brain is awake, patients typically feel happy and unconcerned, but when the right brain is awake, patients tend to feel sad and worried.

Dr. Z's Bookshelf

Caine, Geoffrey and Caine, Renate Nummela. 1991, 1994. *Making Connections: Teaching and the Human Brain.*

Caine, Geoffrey and Caine, Renate Nummela. 1997. *Education on the Edge of Possibility.*

Gamon, David and Bragdon, Allen D. 2000. *Brains that Work a Little Bit Differently: Recent Discoveries About Common Brain Diversities.*

Gardner, Howard. 2004. *Changing Minds: The Art and Science of Changing Our Own and Other People's Minds.*

Gazzaniga, Michael S. 2000. *Cognitive Neuroscience: A Reader.*

Glazer, Steven. 1999. *The Heart of Learning: Spirituality in Education.*

Goleman, Daniel. 1995. *Emotional Intelligence.*

Grandin, Temple and Johnson, Catherine. 2005. *Animals in Translation: Using the Mysteries of Autism to Decode Animal Behavior.*

Hooper, Judith and Teresi, Dick. 1986. *The 3 Pound Universe.*

Howard, Pierce J. 1994. *Applications from Mind-Brain Research.*

Johnson, Steve. 2004. *Neuroscience of Everyday Life.*

Kenyon, Tom. 1994, 2001. *Brain States.*

Kotulak, Ronald. 1996, 1997. *Inside the Brain: Revolutionary Discoveries of How the Mind Works.*

LeDoux, Joseph. 2002. *Synaptic Self: How Our Brains Become Who We Are.*

Majoy, Peter. 1993. *Doorways to Learning: A Model for Developing the Brain's Full Potential.*

Miles, Elizabeth. 1977. *Tune Your Brain: Using Music to Manage Your Mind, Body, and Mood.*

Ornstein, Robert. 1997. *The Right Mind: Making Sense of the Hemispheres.*

Perret, Peter and Fox, Janet. 2004. *A Well-Tempered Mind: Using Music to Help Children Listen and Learn.*

Posner, Michael I. and Raichle, Marcus E. 1994. *Images of Mind.*

Restak, Richard. 2001. *Mozart's Brain and the Fighter Pilot: Unleashing Your Brain's Potential.*

Schiffer, Fredric. 1998. *Of Two Minds: The Revolutionary Science of Dual-Brain Psychology.*

Schmeck, Harold M. and McEwen, Bruce S. 1994. *The Hostage Brain.*

Shaywitz, Sally. 2003. *Overcoming Dyslexia: A New and Complete Science-Based Program for Reading Problems at Any Level.*

Smilkstein, Rita. 2002. *We're Born to Learn: Using the Brain's Natural Learning Process to Create Today's Curriculum.*

Sylvester, Robert. 2000. *A Biological Brain in a Cultural Classroom: Applying Biological Research to Classroom Management.*

West, Thomas G. 1977. *In the Mind's Eye: Visual Thinkers, Gifted People with Dyslexia and Other Learning Difficulties, Computer Images, and the Ironies of Creativity.*

Zull, James. 2002. *Teachers and the Art of Changing the Brain.*

Web Resources

Google Scholar indexes the full-text of scholarly literature. It includes most peer-reviewed online journals of the world's largest scientific publishers. Click on Scholar and then type in your search term followed by filetype:pdf. For example, type "dyslexia filetype:pdf" for articles on dyslexia. **http://scholar.google.com**

Brain Maps is a sophisticated atlas and is not for casual consumption. **http://brainmaps.org**

Brain Briefings is a series of two-page newsletters from the Society for Neuroscience explaining how basic neuroscience discoveries lead to clinical applications. **http://web.sfn. org/index.cfm?pagename=brainBriefin gs_chrolongical** (yes, you have to misspell "chronological")

Brain Child, the MRI study funded by the National Institutes of Health, focuses on how the brain develops in normal, healthy children. **http:// www.brain-child.org**

The Whole Brain Atlas includes neuroimaging of normal and diseased brains. **http://www.med. harvard.edu/AANLIB/home.html**

Digital Anatomist Project includes 2-D and 3-D views of the brain from cadaver sections, MRI scans, and computer reconstructions. **http:// www9.biostr.washington.edu/da.html**

Brain Explorer is a graphical and educational presentation of the brain and the disorders affecting it from the Lundbeck Institute. **http:// www.cnsforum.com**

The Dana Foundation offers news about the brain from many different sources. **http://dana. org**

Songs for Teaching offers music and lyrics on a variety of subjects. **http://www. songsforteaching.com/guffee/mean.htm**

Optical Illusions and Visual Phenomena features 75 fascinating examples. **www. michaelbach.de/ot/index.html**

New Horizons for Learning includes a number of strategies for teachers. **http://www. newhorizons.org/nhfl/about/mission.html**

Cardboard Cognition is a sourcebook of ideas for educational card and board games. **http://edweb.sdsu.edu/courses/edtec670/ Cardboard/CardboardCognition.html**

Brainy Kids (on the Dana site) has links to many stimulating activities about the brain. **http://dana. org/resources/brainykids**

Exploratorium includes fascinating activities on memory. **http://www.exploratorium.edu/ memory**

Brains Rule features activities for students and lesson plans for teachers (lower grades). **http:// www.brainsrule.com**

Neuroscience for Kids has lessons for making 3-D models of neurons, brain games, experiments, worksheets, and more. **http://faculty. washington.edu/chudler/experi.html**

How the Brain Works (for children) **http:// health.howstuffworks.com/brain10.htm**

My Body (entertaining but noisy) **http:// kidshealth.org/kid/body/mybody_SW.html**

Probe the Brain **http://www.pbs.org/wgbh/ aso/tryit/**

Brain Connection: Click on "Games" under "Play" for some delightful tests of short term memory, processing speed, and reaction time. **http://www.brainconnection.com**

Web Resources (cont'd)

PBS Series: "The Secret Life of the Brain" **http://www.pbs.org/wnet/brain**

PBS Scientific American Frontiers: "Changing Your Mind" **http://www.pbs.org/saf/1101**

PBS Scientific American Frontiers: "Hidden Motives" **http://www.pbs.org/saf/1507**

PBS Scientific American Frontiers: "Make Up Your Mind" **http://www.pbs.org/saf/1302**

PBS Scientific American Frontiers: "Don't Forget" **http://www.pbs.org/saf/1402**

PBS Nova Online: "Secrets of the Mind" **http://www.pbs.org/wgbh/nova/mind**

Glossary

amygdala—(plural amygdalae) you have two of these small, almond-shaped groups of neurons located deep inside the temporal lobes. They play a role in the processing of memories and emotional reactions.

articulatory loop—acts as an "inner voice" and repeats a series of words (or other speech elements) on a loop to prevent them from decay.

axon—a long, slender fiber extending from a neuron that conducts nerve impulses away from the body of the cell to a synapse.

brain stem—the part of the brain that connects the spinal cord to the forebrain and cerebrum.

Broca's area—an area of the frontal lobe of the brain associated with the control of speech.

cerebellum—(Latin for "little brain") located between the brainstem and the cerebrum, it plays an important role in sensory perception, motor output, balance, and posture.

cerebral cortex—the grey, folded, outermost layer of the brain that is responsible for higher brain processes such as sensation, voluntary muscle movement, thought, reasoning, and memory.

cognitive load—the amount of effort and fuel utilized by the brain to do a task. The more difficult a task, the greater the cognitive load. Something that you can now do without thinking about it, like driving a car or riding a bicycle does not create a heavy cognitive load. But learning a new skill or concept uses more fuel and activates a larger area of the brain, creating more cognitive load.

cognitive neuroscience—the study of the brain biology that underlies mental processes. Dr. Z is a cognitive neuroscientist. She specializes in neuro-

developmental language disorders and is starting a new research program on the biology of stress. Cognitive neuroscience is one type of neuroscience. Neuroscience is not limited to the brain as we talk about it in this workbook, but covers thousands of topics dealing with cells in the bodies of humans, animals, and insects.

corpus callosum—the large white matter structure that allows interhemispheric transfer; links the left brain to the right brain.

dendrite—slender projection of a neuron that conducts nerve impulses from a synapse to the body of the cell.

episodic memory—a type of long-term memory in which we store memories of personal experiences that are tied to particular times and places. Subcategory of declarative memory.

firing—this takes place when a neuron transmits information to another neuron.

glial cells—(plural glia, Greek for "glue") one of two main types of cells in the nervous system, glial cells provide support and nutrition, maintain homeostasis, form myelin, and participate in signal transmission in the nervous system.

gray matter—(colloquial for "brain") neuroanatomy term for a collection of cell bodies and their dendritic connections; neurons; contrast with white matter

hemispheres—neuroanatomical term for the two halves of the brain; delineated by the body's median plane and connected by the corpus callosum.

Heschl's gyrus—located in the primary auditory cortex, this area processes incoming auditory information.

Glossary (cont'd)

hippocampus—(plural hippocampi) named for its resemblance to a seahorse when viewed from the front, this crescent-shaped part of the limbic system plays a role in long-term memory. You have two them, one on either side, deep inside the temporal lobes.

hypothalamus—a region of the brain located below the thalamus that regulates body temperature, is involved in some metabolic processes, and governs the autonomic nervous system.

lateralization—localization of a function, such as speech, to the right or left side of the brain.

limbic system—part of the human brain involved in emotion, motivation, and emotional association with memory.

lobes—divisions of the cerebral cortex, including the frontal, temporal, parietal, and occipital lobes.

motor cortex—at the back of the frontal lobes, controls movement

neocortex—the top layer of the cerebral hemispheres in the brains of mammals.

neurogenesis—the birth of neurons. Most active during pre-natal development, neurogenesis occurs throughout adulthood.

neuroimaging—uses various technologies to image the structure and function of the brain; includes MRI, fMRI, CT, EEG, MEG, PET, and SPECT, among others (see page 12).

neuronal network—the group of neurons connected by dendrites and axons that is activated by a word, thought, sight, etc. Students grow new neuronal networks when they create a new pathway in the brain by linking neurons together in a new way through learning or engaging in new activities. It is effortful to create this new pathway.

neuron—one of two main types of cells in the nervous system.

neurotransmitter—a chemical messenger that enables neurons to pass signals to each other

plasticity—the ability of the brain to change as a result of experience or learning.

pruning—a process in the brain whereby connections that have not been utilized are reabsorbed by the brain to be used elsewhere.

self-efficacy—an impression that one is capable of performing in a certain manner or attaining certain goals.

semantic memory—a subcategory of declarative memory, semantic memory stores general information such as names and facts.

sensory cortex—at the front of the parietal lobe, it is the receptive area for the sense of touch.

synapse—the junction between the terminal of a neuron and another neuron over which nerve impulses pass.

thalamus (plural thalami)—either of two large, oval-shaped masses of neurons within the forebrain that relay sensory impulses to the cerebral cortex.

Wernicke's area—an area in the brain where the temporal and parietal lobes meet that is responsible for language comprehension. It is connected to Broca's area by a neural pathway called the arcuate fasciculus.

white matter—glial cells, contrast with gray matter

What the research says

Do you have trouble getting students to turn in their homework assignments? Research has shown that writing down when and where you will complete a task increases the probability of follow-through. Doing this sets an **intention** in the brain and the brain is designed for action. Setting an intention serves two purposes. First, it connects the action of carrying out the task to a specific situation (the where and when), thereby creating contextual memory. When the situation is encountered, it serves as a cue to complete the task. Second, it provides a bridge from more abstract to more concrete aspects of the goal.

Get students to make a commitment

Sample strategy

You can use the "Intention" form on the flipside of this page to assign a task. If possible, give students the choice of a two-day turnaround instead of the usual next-day deadline. This gives students more control, creates less anxiety, and allows for students who participate in extracurricular activities or have jobs.

How I will apply this research

Use this space to write your own intention:

_____

_____

_____

_____

Feedback loop: Use the chart below to track your results.

Subject:																							Period:	
Date Due→		BASELINE							INTERVENTION																

Students Turning in Homework

| 36 |
| 32 |
| 28 |
| 24 |
| 20 |
| 16 |
| 12 |
| 8 |
| 4 |

How do you feel about the results of your intervention?

_____

_____

CEU: Use the chart above to track your results and submit

INTENTION

Assignment:

_____

_____

_____

Date due:

_____ / _____ / _____

Date you will complete:

_____ / _____ / _____

Describe the location where you will do the assignment:

_____

_____

_____

Time of day you will begin:

_____ : _____ AM/PM

Signature:

_____

INTENTION

Assignment:

_____

_____

_____

Date due:

_____ / _____ / _____

Date you will complete:

_____ / _____ / _____

Describe the location where you will do the assignment:

_____

_____

_____

Time of day you will begin:

_____ : _____ AM/PM

Signature:

_____

INTENTION

Assignment:

_____

_____

_____

Date due:

_____ / _____ / _____

Date you will complete:

_____ / _____ / _____

Describe the location where you will do the assignment:

_____

_____

Time of day you will begin:

_____ : _____ AM/PM

Signature:

_____

What the research says

Emotion and cognition are linked in the brain. Learning is state dependent. It is affected by your emotional state and that state can be mediated with music. Using music carefully as a tool, you can enhance learning through the creation of a positive emotional state. Violent or aggressive music is *not* appropriate. You the teacher should choose the music as a *tool*. Students can play music of *their* choice on their own time. This isn't playtime: it is using music to create an emotional state conducive to learning and social bonding.

Set the right tone up front

Sample strategy

Find a piece of music suitable for opening music to be played as students enter the classroom. Used for this purpose, it can have words. The words should be positive and the song choice should contribute to a team-building effect. Remember you might not want it to be too arousing (or too relaxing), although a little arousal or stimulation might be good used for this purpose. Play the music for five minutes, or until the bell rings. Students should be in their seats with their pencils sharpened and their materials ready when the music ends. See the flipside for suggested music selections.

How I will apply this research

OPENING MUSIC SELECTION: _____

What I did before:

_____

_____

_____

_____

_____

_____

_____

What I'll do now:

_____

_____

_____

_____

_____

_____

_____

Feedback Loop

What worked:

_____

_____

_____

_____

What I'll do differently next time:

_____

_____

_____

_____

CEU: *Go to Amazon.com and find the selections from Dr. Z's Jukebox on the back of this sheet. Click on the picture of the CD, then "Listen to Samples." Write a brief description and your reaction in the spaces provided. Submit with this page.*

DR. Z'S JUKEBOX FOR OPENING MUSIC

1988 Summer Olympics Album: One Moment in Time

Your Review: _____

_____

_____

Boundless

Relaxed jazz by Scott Wilkie

Your Review: _____

_____

_____

Emerald Castles

Richard Searles

Your Review: _____

_____

_____

We Are Family

Sister Sledge

Your Review: _____

_____

_____

Dance of the Renaissance

by Richard Searles

Your Review: _____

_____

_____

Celebrate

Kool and the Gang

Your Review: _____

_____

_____

Ventana al Sol

South American melodies and rhythms by Echoes of the Incas

Your Review: _____

_____

_____

Summon the Heroes

John Williams, Boston Pops Orchestra

Your Review: _____

_____

_____

The Four Seasons

Vivaldi

Your Review: _____

_____

_____

Unity: The Official Athens 2004 Olympic Games Album

Your Review: _____

_____

_____

What the research says

"Cells that fire together wire together" is known as the Hebbian law. The more a group of neurons fire together, the more likely they are to wire together. Therefore, you want to build repetition of information into lessons. The goal is automaticity—when the knowledge becomes automatic and fluently recalled. All the repetition would not take place in one sitting—learners need time for consolidation. Based on this brain principle, students are more likely to learn material if the network has fired repeatedly. Therefore you will want to design lessons that include repetition in class and as homework.

Use repetition to wire what you've fired!

Sample strategy

As an example, imagine that you are teaching a lesson in which students must memorize the six stages of some event or process. The first repetition is their first exposure to the information. It is more helpful if this initial exposure includes the teacher's pronunciation of key words rather than as silent reading during homework. A second repetition would be when the student reads the material as homework. The next day you might use one of the many ideas in this workbook (Slide Show, Stand Up and Explain, Take a Stand, etc). A fourth repetition could be creating or completing a graphic organizer. Think of ways you can build repetition into an upcoming lesson. The more times the better! Remember to use different modalities. Think of ways to get the students to read it, write it, and say it. Using the form on the reverse, describe in detail how each repetition will be performed. Would this be a good boilerplate plan of action for future lessons? Could it become a procedure in your class? Think homework assignments as well.

How I will apply this research

LESSON TOPIC: _____

What I did before:

_____

_____

_____

What I'll do now:

_____

_____

_____

Feedback Loop

What worked:

_____

_____

_____

What I'll do differently next time:

_____

_____

_____

CEU: Complete the worksheet on the back and submit along with this page.

WIRE WHAT YOU'VE FIRED

1st Repetition	**Modality:** _____ **Description:** _____ _____ _____
2nd Repetition	**Modality:** _____ **Description:** _____ _____ _____
3rd Repetition	**Modality:** _____ **Description:** _____ _____ _____
4th Repetition	**Modality:** _____ **Description:** _____ _____ _____
5th Repetition	**Modality:** _____ **Description:** _____ _____ _____

What the research says

Music is a powerful tool for learning. Combine that with the brain's powerful visual processing and you can have a very powerful tool for the classroom. While some recent research supports the Mozart effect, in which highly complex music enhances spatial/temporal performance, this was a short-term effect and does not have a direct link to classroom practice at this time. However, Mozart is pleasurable and relaxing. Playing appropriate background music (60–80 beats per minute—heartbeat rate—without words) may help students relax and focus on material that can be learned visually.

Enhance visual-spatial processing with music

Sample strategy

For a change of pace, and to add to repetition, try using a slide show with Mozart music in the background. Information that is spatial/temporal would be ideal for this activity, although you could use it for vocabulary practice or memorizing other information. Examples of learning that is spatial/temporal would be visual memory involving location. Learning geography, anatomy, parts of an engine, the location of planets in the solar system, and the names of geometric figures are examples of visual spatial-temporal learning. You can play Mozart quietly in the background while students relax and look at the material, visualizing it while listening to the music. An outstanding way to do this is to make a PowerPoint slide show that plays the music in the background while showing the material to be recalled. Directions for doing this slide show are on the back of this sheet.

How I will apply this research

LESSON TOPIC: _____

What I did before:

_____

_____

_____

_____

_____

_____

What I'll do now:

_____

_____

_____

_____

_____

_____

Feedback Loop

What worked:

_____

_____

_____

What I'll do differently next time:

_____

_____

_____

CEU: *Submit a CD of your PowerPoint presentation or handouts of the visual material that you had students study and the name of the piece of music that you utilized.*

CREATING A POWERPOINT SLIDE SHOW

First scan all pictures you want to use into your computer
Open PowerPoint
Open New Presentation
Slide Layout
Insert picture
Continue inserting pictures into slides until you have your slide show
Insert text as necessary into the slides

Under "Slide Show" choose
"Set Up Show" and
☑ Loop continuously until "Esc"

Under "Slide Show" choose
"Slide Transition" and
Advance slide
☑ Automatically after
00:03
(start with 3 seconds and adjust as needed)

Apply to All

You can either play the CD simultaneously or
Save the music to your computer
Insert Sound
Sound starts automatically
Loop until stopped

What the research says

Sensing progress is HUGE in education, according to James Zull (see Dr. Z's bookshelf). A feeling of progress is what motivates us to persist in tasks that we don't particularly enjoy, such as dusting or mowing the lawn. If we didn't see any difference, would we do it? This is what also keeps us engaged as we learn a difficult sport or hobby. It is rewarding to the brain.

> *"Progress is huge"*
> *James Zull*

Sample strategy

It might follow from this that sensing progress would be motivating to students and keep them engaged. Here is a HUGE challenge for you! As Rita Smilkstein says, "See if you can figure this out!" How can you create a system that shows students their progress? Keep in mind, not *grades* (performance), but *progress*—movement toward a specific goal. First you would have to have a goal, something that could be reached gradually over a period of time. Secondly, that goal would have to be *measurable*. If you can't measure it or observe it, how would students experience the sense of progress? Think: How do you get a sense of accomplishment during your day or week or month? You would want to keep the progress private, unless it was a class goal. I am not going to give an example, because you can come up with something more creative and relevant to your studies, rather than incorporating my generic goal.

Here are some questions to get you started.

- What is your goal?
- How would you measure this?
- How would you or the students track this?

How I will apply this research

GOAL: _____

What I did before:

_____

_____

_____

_____

_____

What I'll do now:

_____

_____

_____

_____

_____

Feedback Loop

What worked:

_____

_____

_____

What I'll do differently next time:

_____

_____

_____

CEU: *Turn in the front and back of this sheet. This one is worth THREE credits.*

PROGRESS CHART

Student Names																	

What the research says

The frontal cortex mediates processes known as "executive functions." Think of what an executive does: planning, prioritizing, using good judgment, evaluating consequences, thinking before speaking, and controlling emotions. The frontal cortex is the executive in the brain. It is the last part of the brain to develop and it continues to develop into young adulthood. In fact, the part responsible for judgment isn't complete until 18–25 years of age. Teachers can help students develop the frontal cortex by providing them with opportunities to use this part of their brain. The older your students, the more you want to focus on these kinds of activities.

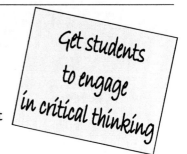
Get students to engage in critical thinking

Sample strategy

See Bloom's Taxonomy on the reverse for words that will help you focus on creating questions and activities that engage the frontal cortex. Students are hesitant to ask or answer this type of question in class and may have very little experience in thinking or talking in that manner. One idea is to do a question or comment grab bag or switch. Students write down their question and then the questions are put into a bag, passed around, and someone else draws and reads the question or statement aloud.

How I will apply this research

LESSON TOPIC: _____

What I did before:

_____

_____

_____

_____

_____

_____

_____

What I'll do now:

_____

_____

_____

_____

_____

_____

_____

Feedback Loop

What worked:

_____

_____

_____

_____

What I'll do differently next time:

_____

_____

_____

_____

CEU: *Complete this worksheet and submit along with questions.*

HIGHER ORDER THINKING SKILLS

Analysis	Synthesis	Evaluation
Identify parts and see repeated order	Put parts together to form a new whole	Judge value or use based on criteria

Analysis	Synthesis	Evaluation
• Analyze	• Test	• Support
• Calculate	• Arrange	• Appraise
• Appraise	• Compare	• Assess
• Contrast	• Compose	• Choose
• Deduce	• Create	• Criticize
• Experiment	• Devise	• Estimate
• Question	• Discuss	• Judge
• Differentiate	• Hypothesize	• Predict
• Discriminate	• Organize	• Select
• Distinguish	• Prepare	• Value
• Dissect	• Report	• Argue
• Categorize	• Schematize	• Attach
• Compare	• Diagram	• Compare
• Criticize	• Write	• Defend
• Examine	• Assemble	• Evaluate
• Investigate	• Collect	• Justify
• Inspect	• Construct	• Rate
• Search	• Design	
• Scrutinize	• Develop	
• Organize	• Formulate	
	• Manage	
	• Plan	
	• Propose	
	• Set up	

From Bloom's Taxonomy

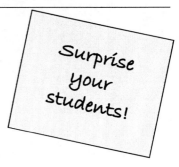

What the research says

Novelty can be both good and bad. It is arousing and engages attention. However, if the situation is stressful, such as testing, a novel environment, for example, can increase the stress. It increases the cognitive load, as it takes some resources to attend and orient to the novel environment or novel social group. On the other hand, novelty in the classroom in a non-stressful situation can positively engage emotion and attention. Do not change where students sit to be novel. People feel strongly about having a "place."

Sample strategy

Having something new and maybe unusual in the room or on your desk can increase interest. Better yet, starting off the day, class or lesson with a totally surprising approach can be very positive. This takes creativity on your part, but is also stimulating for your brain as you create and execute something novel. Recall that by doing something in a different way, you can grow new pathways in your own brain. Don't mention anything to the students—just do it, so they never know what might happen. See the back of this sheet for a few examples of ways you can surprise your students. Use the format to brainstorm some ideas of your own. Caution: don't do anything that would keep them "off-balance."

How I will apply this research

Describe 3 ways you will surprise your students.

SURPRISE #1: _____

_____

SURPRISE #2: _____

_____

SURPRISE #3: _____

_____

Feedback Loop

How did students react? Were they more attentive? Did you feel less stressed?

_____

_____

_____

_____

_____

CEU: *Use the brainstorming form on the back to come up with ways to surprise your students. Then, choose at least 3 surprises and implement them. Complete both sides of this page and submit.*

ABC BRAINSTORMING: SURPRISE YOUR STUDENTS

A	**B** Bring in a caged pet such as a bird or a hamster (even if you have older students—just have it sitting there)	**C** Close the blinds (or open them if they're usually closed)
D Declare a special day, such as "Silent Day" (only writing is permitted) or "Back to Preschool Day" (color and sing)	**E**	**F**
G Go for a walk outside with your students	**H**	**I**
J	**K**	**L**
M	**N**	**O**
P Put a piece of candy on each student's desk	**Q**	**R** Remove everything from the walls and put up a "Coming Soon" sign that is a tease about something they will learn or do
S Sing everything you say (don't say—or sing—too much)	**T** "Top Secret" box (inside can be the homework assignment you distribute at the end of class)	**U**
V	**W** Wear a hat (no reason, just "felt like it")	**XYZ**

What the research says

Because learning involves making connections, it isn't something easily done in isolation. Putting new information into context activates networks related to the context. New information will fire and wire with the existing information. Therefore, lessons should include the "big picture." That is, they should be taught in relation to the bigger context. Make them relate to real life as much as possible.

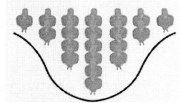

Help students see the big picture

Sample strategy

For your next lesson, determine how you can relate the material to real life. Remember, the students can do the relating as well. If you are teaching the bell curve, line students up by height, then group them into rows (for example, 4'6"–4'8", 4'9"–4'11", 5'–5'2", 5'3"–5'5", 5'6"–5'8", 5'9"–5'11", 6'–6'2") and have them line up, one in front of the other against a wall. The lines in the middle should extend the farthest out and it should look like a bell curve. If you are teaching statistics, don't start with an example from the book. Have students collect information they might be interested in (who uses My Space vs. Face Book—let them pick a topic) and collect from friends and family. Work with these real statistics. Math is easy to apply to real life—not just by using those word problems, but by bringing in a big cookie/cake and cutting it into fractions—using a word problem as a model (If Joe has twice as much as Suzy and Suzy has ¼ of the cake, etc.). Alternately, take students on a field trip prior to teaching and relate the lesson back.

How I will apply this research

LESSON TOPIC: _____

What I did before:

_____

_____

_____

_____

What I'll do now:

_____

_____

_____

_____

Feedback Loop

What worked:

_____

_____

_____

What I'll do differently next time:

_____

_____

_____

CEU: Plan a unit involving real-life activities. Explain how you will make the connections. Discuss how you will address the issue of how individual students' neuronal networks (prior knowledge) will vary and how your lesson will serve as a bridge.

PLANNING PAGE

Objectives:

_____
_____
_____
_____
_____
_____
_____
_____
_____
_____
_____
_____
_____

Plan of Action:

_____
_____
_____
_____
_____
_____
_____
_____
_____
_____
_____
_____

Materials:

_____
_____
_____
_____
_____
_____
_____
_____
_____
_____
_____
_____

Tasks:

_____
_____
_____
_____
_____
_____
_____
_____
_____
_____
_____
_____
_____

What the research says

The more pathways that are activated by new information, the easier the information will be to understand and recall. In addition, you will be more likely to reach students who may learn differently. Remember that we want to create rich, multisensory experiences, activate multiple pathways, create neuronal networks that connect to prior knowledge, and make recall easier.

Create a multisensory environment

Sample strategy

Select an upcoming lesson or unit. How many ways can you think of to present this information? That is your challenge for today. How can you present the information more visually, auditorially, and physically than you did before? How can students manipulate the material? How can you incorporate movement? Think true/false questions for a pretest where one side of the room represents true and the other side false and students move from side to side according to their answers. You can use any dichotomy, such as positive/negative, never/always, subject/verb.

How I will apply this research

LESSON TOPIC: _____

What I did before:

_____

_____

_____

_____

_____

_____

_____

What I'll do now:

_____

_____

_____

_____

_____

_____

_____

Feedback Loop

What worked:

_____

_____

_____

_____

What I'll do differently next time:

_____

_____

_____

_____

CEU: Answer the questions on the back and submit both sides of this sheet.

ACTIVATE MULTIPLE PATHWAYS

What lesson will you use and how did you teach it before? Be specific and describe the steps you took and the way you presented the material.

_____

_____

_____

Visually	How can you present the information more *visually* than you did before?

_____

_____

_____

_____

Auditorially	How can you present the information more *auditorially* than you did before?

_____

_____

_____

_____

Kinesthetically	How can you present the information more *kinesthetically* than you did before? How can they manipulate the material?

_____

_____

_____

_____

Physically	How can you incorporate more *movement*?

_____

_____

_____

What the research says

The brain is primed for pattern-seeking. In fact, pattern detection activates pleasure pathways in the brain, such as when you complete a jigsaw puzzle. To motivate students and keep them from being bored, activate the brain's natural pattern-seeking mechanism.

Activate the pleasure pathway!

Sample strategy

To activate the pattern detection mechanism, phrase a lesson as a puzzle. One easy, fun way to do that is to send students on a "treasure hunt" for something that resembles a concept you are presenting. Announce the treasure hunt before presenting the concept. Ask them to find something in their environment that resembles the concept *in some way* and be prepared to share that verbally or in writing. It may come from TV, radio, or any experience or object in their environment. Then require students to give that information verbally or in writing. Here are some examples:

- o   Find a situation in which you would use this formula: $a^2 + b^2 = c^2$
- o   Find something that is like the structure of an atom (a fan)
- o   Find something that is a kind of summary

How I will apply this research

LESSON TOPIC: _____

What I did before:

_____

_____

_____

_____

_____

_____

_____

What I'll do now:

_____

_____

_____

_____

_____

_____

_____

Feedback Loop

What worked:

_____

_____

_____

_____

What I'll do differently next time:

_____

_____

_____

_____

CEU: *Utilize this strategy in 3 lessons. Provide this sheet for each lesson, along with a list of sample student responses.*

TEACHER QUIZ: PATTERN DETECTION

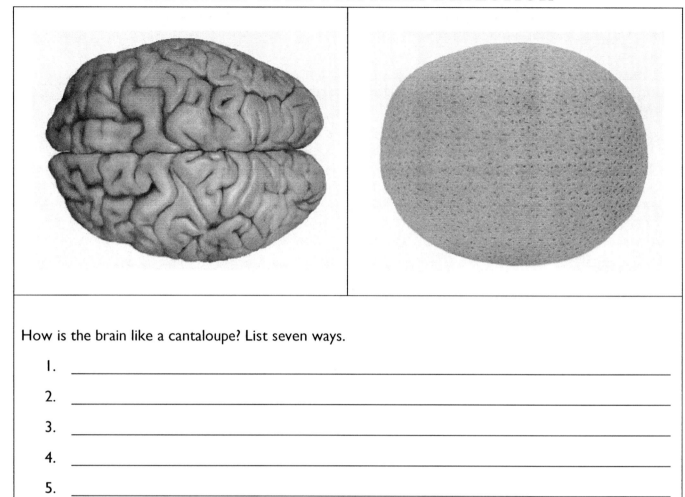

How is the brain like a cantaloupe? List seven ways.

1. _____

2. _____

3. _____

4. _____

5. _____

6. _____

7. _____

Copyright ©2008 Janet N. Zadina, Ph.D. | BR&IN | jzadina@uno.edu

What the research says

You now understand the importance of activating the frontal lobes and helping students think and articulate their thoughts. Talking activates the frontal lobes. Students need to practice articulating their answers and assembling their memories. Students have to wire their ability to actually express an idea as well as to remember it silently. Have you ever heard a student say, "I know it, but I can't explain it?" They have not formed that expressive network yet. It will also be formed through practice.

Don't omit the articulatory loop!

Sample strategy

How can you build more student talk time into a lesson? Describe as many ways as you can to get students speaking aloud in an upcoming lesson. Can they speak to others outside the classroom? As an assignment, pick a concept or process you want students to recall. Have students tell a parent or someone else and have that person write down what the student says and sign the sheet (see reverse). Have the student turn this in.

How I will apply this research

LESSON TOPIC:_____

What I did before:

_____

_____

_____

_____

_____

_____

_____

What I'll do now:

_____

_____

_____

_____

_____

_____

_____

Feedback Loop

What worked:

_____

_____

_____

_____

What I'll do differently next time:

_____

_____

_____

_____

CEU: *Do the selected strategy. Submit this sheet along with a written statement of the assignment.*

HEARSAY INTERVIEW

This assignment gives students practice articulating, or talking about, what they know. The teacher prepares an interview question, such as "Describe the water cycle ..." A parent or other person (interviewer) asks the interview question. The student (interviewee) answers the interview question aloud while the interviewer takes notes.

Student's name (interviewee): _____ Date: _____

Interview question (provided by the teacher):

_____

_____

_____

_____

Name of person interviewing student: _____

Transcription of what the student said (written by interviewer):

_____

_____

_____

_____

_____

_____

_____

_____

_____

_____

_____

_____

_____

_____

_____

_____

Signature: _____

What the research says

Social interaction is positive to the brain. Working in groups elicits cooperation, a state that activates the reward pathway. However, shifts in group membership can be stressful and may negatively affect neurotransmitters, as seen in primate studies where reorganization of social groups affected the levels of serotonin and dopamine. Stable communities reduce stress and make social interaction more positive. On the other hand, occasionally you may want to switch group members around so they can share ideas. Just keep in mind it is fine to do it for a purpose, but not just arbitrarily. Of course, sometimes due to group conflicts, a member might need to move. Be prepared for a temporary disruption before they settle into their new hierarchy.

Provide positive social interaction

Sample strategy

Many opportunities exist to put students into groups to work. However, doing this for its own sake results in strategies in which teachers say "discuss what you read" or "discuss the subject," which often is not productive. Instead, give students a task, such as pattern detection, doing a pretest as a group, listing examples, making individual responses into a polished group response, or working math problems *aloud* as a group. You may want to start with pairs instead of larger groups. The "Think-Pair-Share" format on the reverse will help you get started.

How I will apply this research

LESSON TOPIC: _____

What I did before:

_____

_____

_____

_____

_____

What I'll do now:

_____

_____

_____

_____

_____

Feedback Loop

What worked:

_____

_____

_____

_____

What I'll do differently next time:

_____

_____

_____

_____

CEU: *Turn in this sheet, along with the written assignment sheet that is given to the students for this activity. You may use the form on the reverse if you like.*

THINK-PAIR-SHARE

Question or Problem:

_____

_____

_____

_____

_____

_____

What I thought	**What my partner thought**	**What we decided to share**

THINK-PAIR-SHARE

Question or Problem:

_____

_____

_____

_____

_____

_____

What I thought	**What my partner thought**	**What we decided to share**

What the research says

Learning is about making connections in the brain. Sometimes students have a hard time seeing how material relates to them. Giving them time and the guidance to make these connections is very helpful.

Make connecting statements

Sample strategy

Use the bookmarks on the back as is or adapt them and create your own. Students keep them in their books and can refer to the questions on their own or when designated to do so by you, either in class or for homework. It would be ideal if you laminated them or at least put them on stiffer or colored paper.

How I will apply this research

LESSON TOPIC: _____

What I did before:

_____

_____

_____

_____

_____

_____

_____

_____

What I'll do now:

_____

_____

_____

_____

_____

_____

_____

_____

Feedback Loop

What worked:

_____

_____

_____

_____

What I'll do differently next time:

_____

_____

_____

_____

CEU: *Create a bookmark specifically for your content area. Turn in the bookmark along with this sheet.*

MAKING CONNECTIONS BOOKMARKS

FICTION

This part reminds me of …

I felt like _____ (character) when I …

If that happened to me, I would …

This book reminds me of _____ (another book) because …

I can relate to _____ (part of text) because one time …

Something similar happened to me when …

When I read this part I can close my eyes and picture …

FICTION

This part reminds me of …

I felt like _____ (character) when I …

If that happened to me, I would …

This book reminds me of _____ (another book) because …

I can relate to _____ (part of text) because one time …

Something similar happened to me when …

When I read this part I can close my eyes and picture …

NONFICTION

I have seen something like this before when …

This information reminds me of _____ because…

When I read this information I can close my eyes and picture …

This might affect my life someday because …

I saw a movie that had something like this in it. In the movie …

I can picture myself actually …

If I were the author, I would have explained more about the part …

NONFICTION

I have seen something like this before when …

This information reminds me of _____ because…

When I read this information I can close my eyes and picture …

This might affect my life someday because …

I saw a movie that had something like this in it. In the movie …

I can picture myself actually …

If I were the author, I would have explained more about the part …

What the research says

The brain is plastic, meaning that, like plastic, it can change as a result of experience. The motor strip is especially plastic. The sensory motor strip can change in as few as five days as a result of how it is used. One study showed that learning a piano sequence increased the area in the brain devoted to finger movements as a result of two hours of practice daily for five days. The brain can also change as a result of making connections. Studies pairing sound with a visual showed that after the association was practiced, the visual area would start to respond when it heard the sound associated with that.

So practice does make perfect!

Sample strategy

Do you teach a course that involves motor skills? This strategy would seem to apply more to skills-based courses such as athletics, music, and technical courses. However, keep in mind that pronouncing words involves the motor strip as well. The practicing of saying words aloud can be a valuable strategy. Intense practice of a specific movement will change the brain and make it more likely that the correct movement will occur. You may want to teach children that the brain responds to their practice and that there is a real change in the brain in order to encourage them to practice. Of course, the principle *use it or lose it* applies. Practice must be continued in order to maintain the change. How can you build practice into your curriculum? Students can use the chart on the back to record their practice sessions.

How I will apply this research

LESSON TOPIC: _____

What I did before:

_____

_____

_____

_____

What I'll do now:

_____

_____

_____

_____

Feedback Loop

What worked:

_____

_____

_____

What I'll do differently next time:

_____

_____

_____

CEU: *Submit this page and a daily record of how much practice was done in and out of class.*

DAILY PRACTICE CHART

Name:						Skill:									

Practice Date→	WEEK 1					WEEK 2					WEEK 3				
	M	T	W	T	F	M	T	W	T	F	M	T	W	T	F

 # Repetitions or Minutes: 60, 55, 50, 45, 40, 35, 30, 25, 20, 15, 10, 5

Results:

- -

DAILY PRACTICE CHART

Name:						Skill:									

Practice Date→	WEEK 1					WEEK 2					WEEK 3				
	M	T	W	T	F	M	T	W	T	F	M	T	W	T	F

 # Repetitions or Minutes: 60, 55, 50, 45, 40, 35, 30, 25, 20, 15, 10, 5

Results:

What the research says

Can classical music make children smarter? That notion, known as the "Mozart effect," came to the public's attention in 1993 when Rauscher and Shaw reported that brief exposure to Mozart's piano sonata K 448 produced a temporary increase in spatial reasoning scores, amounting to the equivalent of 8–9 IQ points on the Stanford-Binet (go to my website to hear a sample). Later, the British Epilepsy Organization reported that listening to Mozart's K 448 improved spatial reasoning skills and reduced the number of seizures in people with epilepsy. Scans show that the human brain uses a wide distribution of areas to listen to music. Rhythm and pitch tend to be processed in the left hemisphere, while timbre and melody are processed in the right, unless you are a professional musician, and then the brain treats it differently. Could listening to music prime the parts of the brain that are used for spatial reasoning, resulting in a Mozart effect? Or does music simply produce "enjoyment arousal" as Chabris and Steele argue?

Create a state of relaxed attentiveness

Sample strategy

Play a piece of background music very quietly as students work silently. Remember, for this purpose you want music that is 60-80 beats per minute, similar to the heart rate, and no words. I have found a recording entitled "Celestial Mozart" to be wonderful for creative work. You can go to a music store and ask for functional music or refer to the flipside of this worksheet for suggested titles.

How I will apply this research

TASK MUSIC SELECTION: _____

What I did before:

_____

_____

_____

_____

_____

_____

What I'll do now:

_____

_____

_____

_____

_____

_____

Feedback Loop

What worked:

_____

_____

_____

What I'll do differently next time:

_____

_____

_____

CEU: *Go to Amazon.com and find the selections from Dr. Z's Jukebox on the back of this sheet. Click on the picture of the CD, then "Listen to Samples." Write a brief description and your reaction in the spaces provided. Submit with this page.*

Dr. Z's Jukebox for Task Music

Celestial Mozart
Gerald Jay Markoe

Your Review:_____
_____
_____

Tune Your Brain— Music to Manage Your Mind, Body and Mood
Johann Sebastian Bach …

Your Review: _____
_____
_____

Music for Productivity
Johann Sebastian Bach, Richard Lawrence, Giuseppe Tartini, Georg Philipp Telemann, and Antonio Vivaldi

Your Review:_____
_____
_____

Music for the Mind: Positive Outlook
Various Artists

Your Review: _____
_____
_____

Tune Your Brain with Beethoven: Uplift
José Van Dam, Ludwig van Beethoven …

Your Review: _____
_____
_____

The Yearning Romances for Alto Flute
Michael Hoppe and Tim Wheater

Your Review: _____
_____
_____

Heart Zones
Doc Lew Childre

Your Review: _____
_____
_____

Music for the Mozart Effect: Focus & Clarity
Wolfgang Amadeus Mozart …

Your Review: _____
_____
_____

Smart Symphonies
Various Artists

Your Review: _____
_____
_____

The Spirit Soars
Steve Hall

Your Review: _____
_____
_____

Caution: It is unlikely that listening to these or any other selections will make your students smarter. The purpose of using music in the classroom is to set the optimum emotional tone for the task at hand.

What the research says

Categories are very brain-friendly. While how the brain stores information is not currently well understood, the role of categories in information storage appears strong. The brain categorizes incoming information. Therefore it makes sense that focusing on categories when teaching would be a brain-compatible strategy and would enhance learning.

Sort first, Label later!

Sample strategy

When designing a lesson, determine whether the material easily fits into categories. Then begin a lesson by asking students to work in groups to attempt to categorize. Do not tell them the categories. See if they can determine them through pattern recognition or experience. Using an upcoming lesson, plan for students to categorize the information. Describe the lesson and the anticipated categories. You might have the categories on pieces of paper to have students physically sort them as they work in groups. Some suggestions are

- o   Parts of speech (don't name the categories until afterwards)
- o   Kinds of numbers (even/odd, prime/not prime, whole/fraction)
- o   Cause/Effect
- o   Animate/Inanimate

How I will apply this research

LESSON TOPIC: _____

What I did before: What I'll do now:

_____   _____

_____   _____

_____   _____

_____   _____

_____   _____

Feedback Loop

What worked: What I'll do differently next time:

_____   _____

_____   _____

_____   _____

CEU: Write a description of how you presented the lesson and the specific results. Describe how various groups organized the material. Were students able to determine the categories? Did they understand the material better? Discuss in detail, including the material that was being taught. Submit it with this sheet.

NAME THAT CATEGORY

DIRECTIONS: First sort the words, symbols, or other items. Then name the categories.

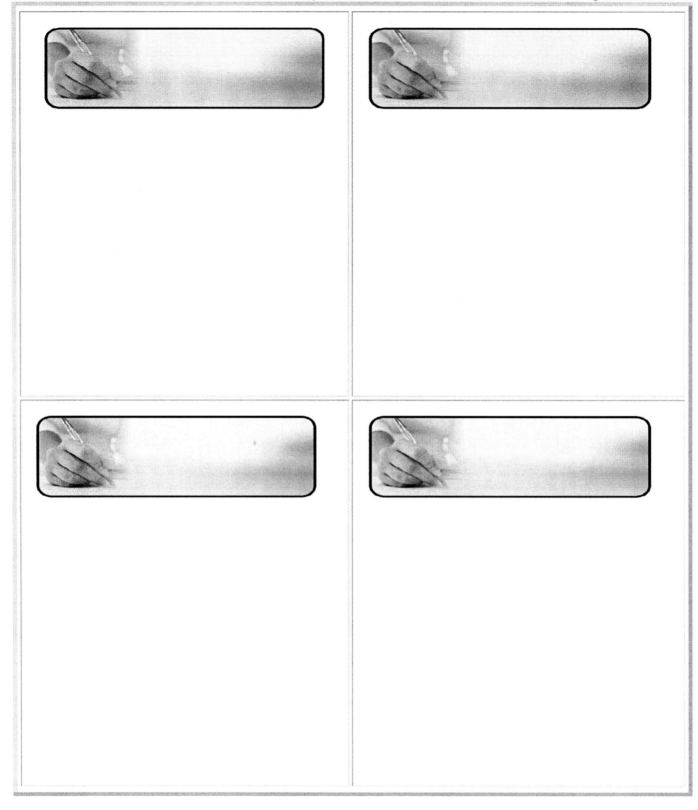

What the research says

Self-efficacy—the belief that one's own actions will produce results—is the focal point of Albert Bandura's social cognitive theory. Self-efficacy is very powerful in setting the right emotional tone and motivating students, because the level of effort your students are willing to expend depends on the results they expect to achieve from their actions. Giving students choices gives them a sense of control, contributing to a sense of self-efficacy. To see research articles on this subject, go to my website at janetzadina.com and click on "Research."

Motivate students by giving choices

Sample strategy

If you get creative, you can think of several ways you can give students a sense of having some control over learning or over outcomes. Can you write extra test questions and ask students to answer three out of four or five out of six? Describe several ways you can offer choice in the classroom. Most of the methods you describe will apply to much of what you teach, so once you write this list you can keep it handy and add these to future lessons. Think way outside the box: can they select their own materials, topics, assignments?

How I will apply this research

LESSON TOPIC: _____

What I did before:

_____

_____

_____

_____

_____

_____

What I'll do now:

_____

_____

_____

_____

_____

_____

Feedback Loop

What worked:

_____

_____

_____

What I'll do differently next time:

_____

_____

_____

CEU: Submit a test in which you have broken the questions down into groups and provided a means for students to select questions. With essay questions, you can give a choice, as well. Include on the test the question "How did you feel taking this test compared to others?" Do not tell the students why you added that. You will cover the directions with students, of course, but don't make an issue of why you are doing something differently. Then, see how students respond. When you submit the test, on the back, write your summary of how students responded.

.

FOUR FACTORS AFFECTING SELF-EFFICACY

According to Albert Bandura's social cognitive theory, four factors affect self-efficacy:

Factor	Self-Talk	Explanation
1. Past Experience	"I've done it before and I can do it again."	Mastery experience is the most important factor affecting a person's self-efficacy. Simply put, success raises self-efficacy, failure lowers it.
2. Modeling	"If they can do it, I can do it, too."	When people see someone succeed at something, their self-efficacy increases; when they see someone fail, their self-efficacy decreases. This is especially true if the model is a peer.
3. Social Persuasions	"If they think I can do it, I probably can."	Social persuasions can have a strong influence on self-efficacy. Encouragement increases self-efficacy; discouragement decreases it. It is easier to decrease someone's self-efficacy than it is to increase it.
4. Physiological Factors	"I can do this, even though my hands are shaking."	Self-efficacy is affected by how a person interprets physiological factors. Trembling hands, nausea, butterflies, etc., may further lower self-efficacy in a person in which it is already low. Those same symptoms in a person with high self-efficacy are most likely to be interpreted as normal and unrelated to his or her ability.

What the research says

Pattern detection is a powerful brain process. Helping students see relationships helps interconnect pathways and is a form of pattern detection. Neurons must connect with other neurons to process information. Helping students make connections helps them process information and connect and fire appropriate neurons to create memories, or neuronal networks.

Teach students to detect relationships

Sample strategy

Have students discuss, write, or draw (*their* option) the relationship between information in a lesson. The act of looking for relationships is rewarding and involves students in making sense of the material. Determine the important relationships (or patterns) in the information you plan to present. Picture how students might see and present the relationship(s). For example, if you are studying parts of speech, ask the students to determine and illustrate the relationship between a subject and a verb. It might be as simple as "the subject usually comes before the verb." They might diagram sentences, list examples in sentences with subject and verb highlighted, or explain it in writing. If you are teaching biology, you might ask what is the relationship of one part of the body to the other parts of the body. In history, you might ask them to show the relationship of economic factors in leading a country to war. In social studies you could ask them to determine the relationship between the senate and house.

How I will apply this research

LESSON TOPIC:_____

What I did before:

What I'll do now:

_____   _____

_____   _____

_____   _____

_____   _____

_____   _____

_____   _____

Feedback Loop

What worked:

What I'll do differently next time:

_____   _____

_____   _____

_____   _____

_____   _____

CEU: *Complete the front and back of this worksheet and submit.*

DETECTING RELATIONSHIPS

The relationship that I want students to see is that between

_____ & _____ .

Show the relationship in ways that represent an "A" response.

Diagram	Examples	Written

Write the assignment here.

_____

_____

_____

_____

_____

_____

_____

Comment on the results.

_____

_____

_____

_____

_____

What the research says

The more pathways students activate, the more pathways they create. If one learns something through more than one sense or type of experience, the more intricate the network will be. It will also be easier to recall the information if it is stored in multiple ways.

Activate multiple pathways!

Sample strategy

Select an upcoming concept or lesson that you plan to teach. How many ways could a student work with it? Be explicit. How many options can you come up with? The ideal situation is to give the students a sheet of options and let them select their homework assignment one day and another day you may assign some of the options to various groups or have them make a second selection, as you continue to work with the topic. List at least 5 ways in the space below. Write your response in the form of an assignment. Think of specific senses, talents, or refer to Howard Gardner's Multiple Intelligences theory.

How I will apply this research

LESSON TOPIC:_____

The options I will offer are:

1. _____

2. _____

3. _____

4. _____

5. _____

Feedback Loop

What worked: What I'll do differently next time:

_____   _____

_____   _____

_____   _____

_____   _____

CEU: *Create at least 5 options for a homework assignment. Turn in both this page and that assignment sheet.*

ACTIVATING MULTIPLE PATHWAYS

Drawing	
Humor	
Drama	
Metaphor	
Speaking	
Visualizing	
Listening	
Hands-on	
Narrative	

What the research says

Neuroimaging studies have shown how effective the brain is at recalling visual information. Capitalizing on the brain's strength in visual processing can help learners. Try to incorporate visual information as much as possible. Tagging visual information to declarative information will make it easier to remember. Everyone benefits from visual imagery and for visual learners, it may be critical.

Tag visual information to declarative

Sample strategy

Complete this statement: A picture is _____ _____ _____ _____.
Although everyone knows this saying, we seem to think pictures are only necessary for elementary materials. But the brain likes images. Go to Google and click on Image. Search for images that illustrate your lesson. Describe what you found and how you will incorporate the images into your lesson. For example, select vocabulary words from your lesson—words that students may not know. Can you find images that illustrate them? For example, if you are talking about a political situation "escalating," find a picture of an escalator to associate with the word and discuss the relationship between the two.

How I will apply this research

LESSON TOPIC:_____

What I did before:

_____

_____

_____

_____

_____

_____

What I'll do now:

_____

_____

_____

_____

_____

_____

Feedback Loop

What worked:

_____

_____

_____

What I'll do differently next time:

_____

_____

_____

CEU: Utilize this sheet for 3 lessons. Provide this sheet for each one.

A PICTURE IS WORTH ...

The Internet offers an all-you-can-download buffet of visual imagery, much of which is free. Just search for images, right click on the image of your choice (in most cases), and save the image to your computer. You can then use the images in PowerPoint presentations, include them in instructional materials, or print them for display.

If you need specific help in working with images, try http://webclipart.about.com/od/tutorialshelp/l/blhelp7.htm . The directions below are from that site.

Download With Internet Explorer (IE)

1. Click on clip art first to see if this brings up a larger image to download.
2. On the larger image, or on the original image, place the cursor on the clip art and RIGHT CLICK with the mouse.
3. This will bring up a small menu. Choose the SAVE PICTURE AS option.
4. Choose a directory/folder in which to place this image.
5. Click SAVE.

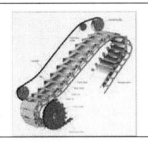	http://images.google.com/ "The most comprehensive image search on the web." The image at left was obtained from that site.
	http://earth.google.com/gallery/ Want to explore the Grand Canyon? It's just a double-click away.
 Image:Dust Bowl - Dallas, South Dakota 1936.jpg From Wikipedia, the free encyclopedia	http://en.wikipedia.org/wiki/Main_Page This free online encyclopedia features downloadable images that accompany the articles.
	http://web.mit.edu/persci/people/adelson/checkershadow_downloads.html What discussion of visual imagery is complete without at least a nod to optical illusions?

What the research says

Inductive or "backwards" teaching means giving students the experience to create a neuronal network before naming a new definition or concept. You use inductive reasoning when you make a hypothesis, formulate a theory, or discover relationships. Inductive reasoning is essential for scientific discovery. You can give students practice using inductive reasoning and stimulate their pleasure pathways as well by providing them with a network to which they can connect the new information. Because the brain must make connections between information in order to create a neuronal network, it is important to help students create this neuronal network. Information that doesn't activate a neuronal network isn't likely to be recalled.

Teach inductive reasoning

Sample strategy

Let's say you're teaching the term *preposition*. Traditionally, you might write the term on the board and give students the definition. The brain-compatible way is to present an array of prepositions and let students discover what they all have in common. In doing so students will create their own definition of what a preposition is. Then there is no need to memorize, as they understand the concept. Once they have the concept, you can name it. This can also be done with math formulas. If you give them enough examples, they can figure out the formula. This strategy is helpful when teaching definitions, formulas, and principles. Use the lesson plan format on the other side of this sheet to prepare a lesson using "backwards" teaching.

How I will apply this research

LESSON TOPIC:_____

Describe any preliminary false conclusions:

_____

_____

_____

_____

_____

_____

Did students reach the correct answer? Elaborate.

_____

_____

_____

_____

_____

_____

Feedback Loop

What worked:

_____

_____

_____

What I'll do differently next time:

_____

_____

_____

CEU: Create and implement a lesson plan that uses "backwards" teaching. Submit along with this sheet.

BACKWARDS TEACHING LESSON PLAN FORMAT

Goal(s) for students to achieve:

_____

_____

Criteria for meeting goal:

_____

_____

_____

Segment 1: Experience to begin creating a neuronal network
(for example: real life experience, pattern detection)

_____

_____

_____

_____

_____

Segment 2: Practice applying the concepts that were discovered

_____

_____

_____

_____

Segment 3: Name the concept for them

_____

- o Provide additional information
- o Provide repetition

Brain-Compatible Strategies:

- ☐ Articulating
- ☐ Brainstorming
- ☐ Drama
- ☐ Drawing
- ☐ Field Trips
- ☐ Games

- ☐ Graphic Organizers
- ☐ Humor
- ☐ Journals, Reflection
- ☐ Manipulatives
- ☐ Metaphor
- ☐ Movement

- ☐ Music
- ☐ Narrative
- ☐ Novelty
- ☐ Pattern Detection
- ☐ Social Interaction
- ☐ Visual images

What the research says

Emotion is critical to learning. *High* stress impairs the kind of learning that we want to do in school. There are more projections *from* the limbic system to the frontal cortex than there are from the frontal cortex to the centers of emotion in the limbic system. Therefore, it is easier for emotions to overcome thinking than for us to use thinking to overcome emotions, especially during times of high stress. Therefore, you want to build ways to reduce stress into your classroom procedures and activities.

Reduce stress with a pretest

Sample strategy

There are several ways to reduce stress. One of those is to provide for non-graded learning and assessment opportunities. One strategy for doing that is to give a pretest. Remember that the goal of testing is to see if they learned it, not to *catch* them not having yet learned it. A pretest gives them a chance to see if they know the material yet. One fun way to do that and to build movement into the classroom is to do the true/false pretest in which the students "Take a Stand," i.e., move to one side of the room for *true* and the other side for *false*. You should also administer a written non-graded assessment. Pretests are only valuable, however, if the students understand the benefits derived from them—that it is not just something to do, but something to *help* them. Determine how you can add a non-graded assessment into your current unit.

How I will apply this research

LESSON TOPIC: _____

What I did before:

_____

_____

_____

_____

_____

_____

What I'll do now:

_____

_____

_____

_____

_____

_____

Feedback Loop

What worked:

_____

_____

_____

_____

What I'll do differently next time:

_____

_____

_____

_____

CEU: *Submit this page, along with the non-graded assessment and the graded assessment.*

EFFECT OF PRETEST ON PERFORMANCE

	Baseline (without pretest)					Intervention (with pretest)				
	A	B	C	D	F	A	B	C	D	F

Number of students achieving grade (vertical axis, values 1–23)

23										
22										
21										
20										
19										
18										
17										
16										
15										
14										
13										
12										
11										
10										
9										
8										
7										
6										
5										
4										
3										
2										
1										

What the research says

Our brains were designed to learn information based on real life experiences, but today we sometimes find it necessary to memorize facts. This is a more difficult task for the brain than remembering events or experiences. It is very difficult if the student has not yet developed neuronal networks (prior knowledge) that support this new information. Learning is based on the ability to make *connections* in the brain. Students must be able to connect this new information to their existing knowledge. You can help them do this.

Give students time to reflect

Sample strategy

While a structured, explicit activity to make connections is best, an option that can be helpful is giving students time to reflect on the material, so that they can find connections. This is best used when you believe that they already have the prior knowledge, but just need to *activate* it. "Log On, Log Off" is a great way to give students time to reflect. Start the class with time for the students to journal about what they already know and end it with time for them to journal about the material that was presented. You can use the form on the back or have them write into a journal or notebook. Give them two minutes at the beginning and two minutes at the end. Their pens must *not* stop the entire time, even if they have to write "blah, blah, blah" until an idea comes to them.

How I will apply this research

LESSON TOPIC: _____

What I did before:

_____

_____

_____

_____

_____

_____

What I'll do now:

_____

_____

_____

_____

_____

_____

Feedback Loop

What worked:

_____

_____

_____

_____

What I'll do differently next time:

_____

_____

_____

_____

CEU: Describe a method other than the "Log On, Log Off" method. Turn in that description along with this page.

LOG ON

Name: _____

_____
_____
_____
_____
_____

LOG OFF

_____
_____
_____
_____
_____
_____

LOG ON

Name: _____

_____
_____
_____
_____
_____

LOG OFF

_____
_____
_____
_____
_____
_____

What the research says

Brain scans have shown that novice learners performing a new task engage many regions of the brain and use more fuel than after the task has become fluent. Once they have achieved automaticity, or become fluent, they activate less brain area and burn less fuel. When the brain is so fully engaged in a new task and it requires much concentration, we call this heavy *cognitive load*. *Cognitive load* can be thought of as the energy or effort required by the brain for a task. The frontal lobes are carrying much of the weight until it becomes automatic and the cerebellum can take some of the load. When you first learned to drive, you experienced heavy cognitive load. You had to fully concentrate and couldn't talk or listen to music. Now, when you drive, you can allocate attention to many other tasks (including some that are not safe, such as text-messaging ☺).

Sample strategy

It can be helpful to reduce cognitive load when students are first learning a task and then increase it as they become more fluent. One way to reduce cognitive load is to teach one skill until students are fluent before moving on to the next skill. That is *ideal* but not always possible. One way to reduce cognitive load is to teach a skill or concept without a heavy dependency on reading and writing until the concept is learned. Then bring in the reading and writing. Another way to encourage fluency is to make a PowerPoint flash card activity. Using the instructions on page 26 for creating a PowerPoint slide show, create a presentation that flashes a question and then the answer using the PP timing feature. So it might flash a math problem and then a pause for students to speak out the answer and then it flashes the answer and they get timely feedback. You can use this with language learning, formula learning, or anything that you want them to automatize.

How I will apply this research

LESSON TOPIC: _____

What I did before: What I'll do now:

_____   _____

_____   _____

_____   _____

_____   _____

Feedback Loop

What worked: What I'll do differently next time:

_____   _____

_____   _____

_____   _____

CEU: *Create the automatic PowerPoint flash cards and submit the presentation along with this sheet.*

To experience cognitive load take the Stroop test for yourself. The Stroop task presents the names of colors written in a color other than the name of that color. The task is to name the colors of words without reading the word. Do the task aloud as quickly as you can. You can locate one version at

http://www.apa.org/science/stroop.html

Interference: The Stroop Effect Don't *read* the words on the right--just *say* the colors they're printed in, and do this aloud as fast as you can. ***You're in for a surprise!*** If you're like most people, your first inclination was to read the words, 'red, yellow, green...,' rather than the colors they're printed in, 'blue, green, red...' You've just experienced *interference*. When you look at one of the words, you see both its *color* and its *meaning*. If those two pieces of evidence are in conflict, you have to make a choice. Because experience has taught you that word meaning is more important than ink color, interference occurs when you try to pay attention *only* to the ink color.	**red** yellow **green** blue red **blue** **yellow** green blue **red**

You can print this out from the website using a color printer or put it on a screen using an overhead or LCD projector and have the students perform the task. Then ask the students if they could feel the extra brain power that it took to do the task. Did they make mistakes? Explain to them that this is what happens when you do a verbal task like your school work with the television or radio on in the background. It is like a computer program with another process running in the background. It slows down your thinking and increases mistakes because it raises the cognitive load.

What the research says

In a study at Howard by Wagner (1998) subjects were more likely to remember words when they focused on their meanings rather than how the words looked, such as spelling. Based on this research, we may want to make sure to mention to students to visualize the meaning of the word. Always keep in mind that one study is simply that, one study, and must be replicated and expanded. Also, the implications are not necessarily direct, but we like to use the studies to try strategies that may be more effective.

Visualize the meanings of words

Sample strategy

Play "Pictionary" with words students need to learn for an upcoming lesson. Give students time to practice drawing a word in a way that has meaning for them. Have volunteers go to the board and recreate their drawings. Then go on to the next word. Write your word list on the back. Try your hand at illustrating all of the words. The drawing may represent how it looks, how it's used, or as part of a bigger picture, anything that brings the meaning to you. Another strategy to incorporate is teaching prefixes, roots, and suffixes. It may seem outdated to you, but it is an excellent strategy. These break words into parts and the parts have meaning, thus activating a network of associated meaning. This strategy applies what was learned in that study.

How I will apply this research

LESSON TOPIC: _____

What I did before:

_____

_____

_____

_____

_____

_____

What I'll do now:

_____

_____

_____

_____

_____

_____

Feedback Loop

What worked:

_____

_____

_____

_____

What I'll do differently next time:

_____

_____

_____

_____

CEU: Complete both sides of this sheet and submit.

"PICTIONARY" CARDS

What the research says

Emotional experiences can create strong memories. The centers for emotion are linked to centers for memory. Strong emotion, both positive and negative, can enhance memories. Of course, we want to use positive emotion. Some positive emotions you may want to elicit are joy, pleasant surprise, appreciation, laughter, tenderness, excitement, intrigue, and compassion.

Use positive emotion to enhance memory

Sample strategy

Bringing in a pet may induce affection, tenderness, or excitement. Starting class with a joke (no sarcasm) can be effective, even if the joke is silly or corny. An ideal way to introduce positive emotion on an ongoing basis is to undertake a community project. My favorite is having the students read to the very young or the elderly in a retirement home. This promotes bonding, pride, compassion, and the feeling of making a contribution.

How I will apply this research

LESSON TOPIC: _____

What I did before:

_____

_____

_____

_____

_____

_____

_____

What I'll do now:

_____

_____

_____

_____

_____

_____

_____

Feedback Loop

What worked:

_____

_____

_____

_____

What I'll do differently next time:

_____

_____

_____

_____

CEU: For 5 credits, undertake a community project. Write up your plan and a description of how it progressed. Assess the outcome and submit. Write "=5 hrs." on your submission.

APT APHORISMS

Half the people you know are below average.

If at first you don't succeed,
destroy all evidence that you tried.

A classic is a book that everybody praises…
and nobody reads.
                              Mark Twain

Don't sweat petty things…
or pet sweaty things.

A conscience is what hurts
when all your other parts feel so good.

A clear conscience is usually the sign of a bad memory.

Did you know that five out of three people
have trouble with fractions?

What the research says

There are several types of memory. When you memorize facts, you are using semantic memory. This is not the easiest memory system in which to move information from working memory to long-term memory. There are two types of memory that are easier to encode and recall. One is procedural memory. This is the kind a healthy brain doesn't forget, such as how to ride a bike or tie your shoes. Another type is episodic memory. Reflect a moment on some memories of when you were in school. Those would be episodic memories. (A profitable exercise would be to journal those memories, see if you can figure out what made them memorable, and try to create that for your students.) One way to turn semantic into procedural or episodic memories is through drama. This may make it easier for students to recall.

Show, don't tell!

Sample strategy

Create positive emotion, episodic memories, and provide for movement in the classroom by incorporating drama or acting. One educational leader fondly recalled when students would mime a process so that the other students would learn to write by "showing" rather than telling, as they wrote down the actions the "mime" performed. Accept volunteers. Not all students are comfortable with this behavior and our goal is positive emotion and learning skills, not making students do something like that. Another way to use drama is to have student role-play, debate issues, or act out a story that was assigned. Find an upcoming lesson that would lend itself to acting on the part of some students. Describe that lesson. This is a great option on your homework assignment sheet as well.

How I will apply this research

LESSON TOPIC: _____

What I did before:

_____

_____

_____

_____

_____

_____

What I'll do now:

_____

_____

_____

_____

_____

_____

Feedback Loop

What worked:

_____

_____

_____

What I'll do differently next time:

_____

_____

_____

CEU: Complete both sides of this sheet and submit.

TURN SEMANTIC INTO EPISODIC MEMORY

Setting
_____
_____
_____
_____
_____

Characters
_____
_____
_____
_____
_____
_____
_____
_____

Problem or Plot
_____
_____
_____
_____
_____
_____
_____
_____
_____

Solution or Ending
_____
_____
_____
_____
_____

What the research says

Singing is more powerful than people realize. For an experience from your life, ask yourself how often you "sing" the ABC song when alphabetizing. You can recall songs from your earliest years. People with Alzheimer's disease can sing songs long after much of their declarative memory is gone. People who stutter usually do not stutter when they sing. Another surprising fact is that some people who have had a stroke and can't speak can sing. There is even some new research that says if you sing-song what you are saying to people with Alzheimer's or Wernicke's aphasia (can't comprehend language) they may be able to understand you. So let's capitalize on this powerful tool.

Use Lyrics for Long-term memory

Sample strategy

I often had students sing in the classroom. If we were doing a reading lesson, I could take appropriate lyrics and put them on an overhead. Those who wanted to, sang, and the rest followed along. It made a great reading lesson. Another way to incorporate song and to get variety into your strategies is to give as a homework choice the option to write song lyrics that review material that has been learned. They would use the melody from a popular song and write their own lyrics. Then the class can sing along as a review. This really helps with new vocabulary as it gives students a chance to engage the articulatory loop and pronounce the new words. It also gives students lots of rehearsal time as they think of the words and try to fit them into the melody. This is a great small group activity as well. As with every assignment, our quality standards are still high.

How I will apply this research

LESSON TOPIC: _____

What I did before:

_____

_____

_____

_____

_____

_____

What I'll do now:

_____

_____

_____

_____

_____

_____

Feedback Loop

What worked:

_____

_____

_____

What I'll do differently next time:

_____

_____

_____

CEU: Submit at least five songs that students have written in your class. You may accumulate these over the course of a semester as few students may choose this option.

SAMPLE LYRICS FROM ONE OF MY WORKSHOPS

To the tune of
Santa Claus is Coming to Town

You better not frown
You better not glare
You better not traumatize
Or scare me, dear
Emotion drives attention to learn

Attention can be captured
Both positive and negative
Excitement registers good or bad
So no looming for heaven's sake.

Ponca City Middle School
Christy, Gail, Amy, Sharron, Deana, Janie, Freda

To the tune of
Row, Row, Row Your Boat

Fire, fire, fire your brain
In your frontal lobe
The more you fire, the more you acquire,
Your brain is like a strobe.

Frontal, frontal, frontal lobe
Learn about what's there.
The reason you hit your friend at lunch,
Your frontal's not quite there.

For 7th graders
Ponca City Middle School
Lora, Heather, Lynetta, Carey, Chaunte, Kassie, Jackie

The Brain Song
To the tune of **The Bone Song**

The brain has a right and a left side
The right helps us learn through our sight
The left uses phonetics with all it's might
And that's how the brain should work.

One brain's motto is connect and reflect
If that doesn't work you can't recollect
If you can't recollect your life's a wreck
And that's how the brain should work.

Ponca City Middle School
Steve Harris, Dianna Monks, Aaron Watson,
Jonathan Baker, Stoney Parks, John Reynolds,
Cynthia Winterrowd, Steve McKay

Born to be Wired
To the tune of **Born to be Wild**

Get your neurons going…
Fire up your dendrites…
Looking for attention
To whatever comes your way…
Born to be wired…
Born to be wired…

Neurons making dendrites
Making good synapses
Using all your glucose
So your learning never lapses
Born to be wired…
Born to be wired….

Ponca City
Middle School
Penny Keller, Linda Cole, Marcia Keathly, Joyce
Mayer, Mark Hodgson, Brian Darnell, Lonnie
Gilliand, Gineta Swanson

To the tune of
99 Bottles of Beer on the Wall

Practice, practice, practice
practice, practice, practice
Use I now and pass it around
Practice, practice, practice

Inductive learning, inductive learning
Use I now and pass it around
Inductive learning

Metaphor, metaphor, metaphor
Metaphor, metaphor, metaphor,
Use I now and pass it around
Metaphor, metaphor, metaphor

Images, images, images,
Images, images, images,
Use I now and pass it around
Images, images, images

Narrative, narrative, narrative,
Narrative, narrative, narrative
Use I now and pass it around
Narrative, narrative, narrative

Ponca City Middle School
Donya, Deb, Marsh, Angela, GayAnn, Susan, Sheila

What the research says

The brain is designed to see patterns, especially deviations from a pattern. This is survival-driven, much as seeing a snake in the leaves, so it is a powerful, natural process. Seeing patterns also activates the reward pathway in the brain, giving pleasure, such as when one completes a crossword puzzle. So it really makes sense to co-opt this process in support of learning.

Puzzle it out with graphic organizers

Sample strategy

Make a graphic organizer that represents relationships in material that you plan to cover in a lesson. Leave enough of the diagram blank for students to fill in. You may have some pre-completed to guide students if necessary. Can you make a graphic organizer for every lesson? Better yet, could your students create one? Select an appropriate template for the material from the examples on the flipside.

How I will apply this research

LESSON TOPIC: _____

What I did before:

_____

_____

_____

_____

_____

_____

_____

_____

What I'll do now:

_____

_____

_____

_____

_____

_____

_____

_____

Feedback Loop

What worked:

_____

_____

_____

What I'll do differently next time:

_____

_____

_____

CEU: *Submit this page, along with the graphic organizer that you designed to support the learning process.*

SAMPLE GRAPHIC ORGANIZERS

Several types of editable graphic organizers are available in Microsoft Word, as shown below (except for the Fishbone). Just click on "Diagram Gallery" in the toolbar, represented by a Cycle icon. Many more are available at http://www.edhelper.com/teachers/General_graphic_organizers.htm.

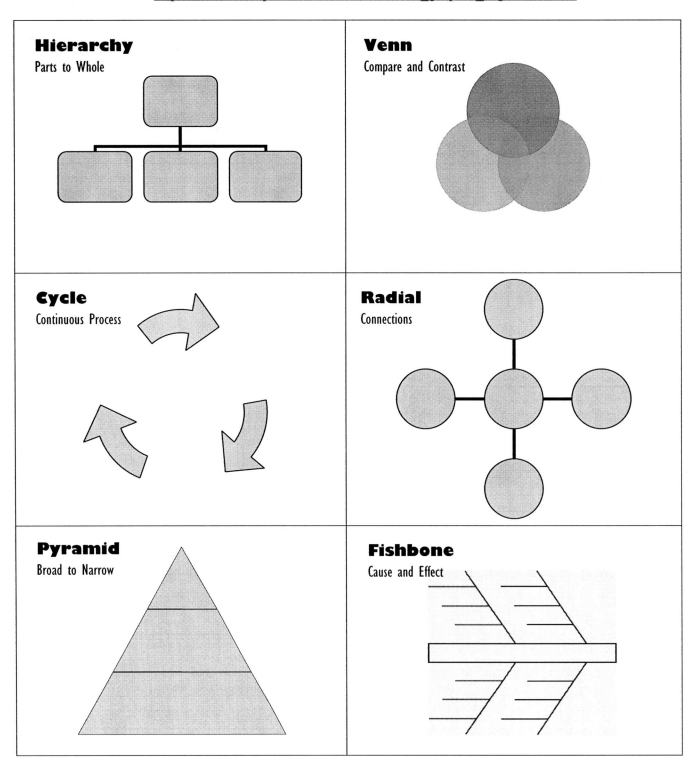

Hierarchy
Parts to Whole

Venn
Compare and Contrast

Cycle
Continuous Process

Radial
Connections

Pyramid
Broad to Narrow

Fishbone
Cause and Effect

What the research says

Memories in the brain are not stored in the manner in which they are on a computer. A computer stores memories in a document file for verbal "memories" or a jpeg for visual "memories." When you call it up, it is the same every time, unless you deliberately change it. However, the brain does not store memories in an intact file. While it is not well understood how memories are stored in the brain, it does seem that the brain has to reassemble the memories from various locations in the brain. Students may comprehend in class and think that they understand the material and can remember it. However, they have not yet practiced *reassembling* their memories, a much more difficult task than comprehension. Have you not heard students say, "I know it, but I can't say it." They have not yet formed the "articulatory loop" or fired the pathway of *reassembling* the material.

Practice reassembling the memory

Sample strategy

There are many ways to give students practice time in reassembling their memories. Stand Up and Explain is excellent because it gives students an opportunity to fire the articulatory loop and actually say the material as well as think it. Having students journal or answer essay questions is another way. Another easy way to build this into your classroom, and accomplish some other important tasks as well, is to have a Ticket Out the Door. Students have to turn in the ticket to leave the classroom. I find it handiest to have a generic ticket (see reverse). On a given day I say "answer #1" or whichever I choose for that day. But if I want them to rehearse the reassembly of *specific* information, I will tell them to turn the ticket over and "explain the process of photosynthesis" or whatever was covered that day. It should be something that they can explain in two or three sentences—in the space on the back of the ticket. This generic ticket allows you to be consistent in requiring it and to set up a procedure. It also allows you to make sure you are checking in with students in a very easy way that doesn't involve grading. You don't even have to read the tickets some days, because the purpose is for them to *experience* reassembling the memory—not for you to grade it. Feel free to stop a student at the door if you glance down and see an incomplete or sloppily done ticket. Send them back to their seat. They will learn that the ticket is an important activity.

How I will apply this research

LESSON TOPIC:_____

What I did before:

What I'll do now:

_____   _____

_____   _____

Feedback Loop

What worked:

What I'll do differently next time:

_____   _____

_____   _____

CEU: *Write out 10 items that you would want students to explain (reassemble their memory) in upcoming lessons.*

TICKET OUT THE DOOR

I didn't understand _____

One new thing I learned was _____

I most enjoyed _____

TICKET OUT THE DOOR

I didn't understand _____

One new thing I learned was _____

I most enjoyed _____

TICKET OUT THE DOOR

I didn't understand _____

One new thing I learned was _____

I most enjoyed _____

Six Weeks to a Brain-Compatible Classroom:
Using Brain Research to Enhance & Energize Instruction

A Workbook for Educators

by JANET N. ZADINA, PH.D.

- Reinforcement of BR&IN key concepts
- Quick reference guide to relevant facts about the brain
- Detailed and illuminating illustrations
- Dozens of ideas for using BR&IN strategies in the classroom
- Glossary of key terms
- Recommended web links
- Bibliography of titles on Dr. Zadina's bookshelf
- Handy forms and masters for executing the strategies
- Optional hand-in assignments for continuing education credits

Her presentation fired it; now her workbook helps you wire it!

NAME _____ DATE _____

E-MAIL ADDRESS _____ PHONE _____

STREET ADDRESS _____

CITY _____ STATE _____ ZIP _____

Workbook: Six Weeks to a Brain-Compatible Classroom	Unit Price	Quantity	Extended Price
Under 75 copies	$10.00		
75–500 copies	9.00		
500–800 copies	8.25		
800+	7.66		
US Postage & Handling (Total) :		1 book: $3.76	
		2-3 books: $4.00	
		4-6 books: $8.00	
		7-9 books: $10.00	
		10 or more books: 10%	
Outside US: email jzadina@uno.edu for arrangements			
		Total Cost	

Mail this order form with your check made payable to:

Janet Zadina

13785 Walsingham Rd. #151

Largo, FL 33774

Please allow approximately two weeks for delivery from the date we receive your order.

BR&IN
BRAIN RESEARCH
and INSTRUCTION